PITTSBURGH MEMORANDA

PITTSBURGH
MEMORANDA
HANIEL LONG

UNIVERSITY OF PITTSBURGH PRESS

Published by the University of Pittsburgh Press, Pittsburgh Pa. 15260
Copyright © 1935, Haniel Long
Copyright © 1990, University of Pittsburgh Press
All rights reserved
Baker & Taylor International, London
Manufactured in the United States of America

Library of Congress Cataloging-in-Publication Data

Long, Haniel, 1888–1956.
  Pittsburgh memoranda / Haniel Long.
    p.   cm.
  ISBN 0-8229-3657-7
  1. Pittsburgh (Pa.)—Poetry.   I. Title.
PS3523.0466P58   1990
811'.52—dc20   90-33956
                                                         CIP

To my wife and son

CONTENTS

Our forefathers were pioneers.
So are we.

They came like shadows through the Alleghenies,
exploring and hoping.

They saw the red azaleas, the white shadbush,
the bloodroots, the Judas trees.

Our forefathers could drive their oxen
through the dangerous mountain valleys.
They could shield their families from savages,
knew how to deal with the wild and strange,
had the points of the compass in their blood.

They built a new city where these rivers meet
and died victorious over the outward.

We live in the homes and the new city they built
and find it none too easy.

They knew the mountains and the midnight skies.
We know chambers filled with talk and silence,
ghosts and hallucinations. We have come
under roofs to a fantastic air, somehow.

Our fathers died victorious over the outward.
Peace to them. Courage to us,
who fight not Indians but insanity.

I

We go quietly; there is much to do,
but nothing to do without going quietly.

Living rooms, bedrooms, court-houses,
banks, asylums,
are no more mysterious than the out of doors;
we shall know them and ourselves who dwell in them,
and what the shapes that dwell in the wilderness
within us all.

The sky is a vast inverted bowl of blue;
about the circling rim the furnaces
are emptying into it like yellow rivers.

We have senses which may lead to trails,
we may find trails which lead to water;
we are making a new compass
from the compasses of yesterday;
even in the fantastic air of chambers,
are feeling our way towards passes through the mountains.

Intrepidity was not interred with our forefathers,
and nothing matters now but finding springs.

Following the elder wisdom we cherish likewise the new;
we stay pioneers, but the trails are leading inwards.

Our forefathers went shadowlike
into beautiful new valleys
of orioles and of rhododendron
—and of death.

Our forefathers went shadowlike
into beautiful dangerous new valleys.

We are their children; we too explore and hope,
making the filaments of a new compass
out of our need to come to terms with ourselves,
with the others who live life with us,
and the life that lives all.

Homestead is almost my first memory.

A July morning of early childhood. I bring in the milk bottles and the morning papers, and across the paper is big black type.

My father starts when he sees the headlines and says to my mother, "Some anarchist has stabbed Clay Frick."

"Men in action are the poet's proper theme."

That spring Andrew Carnegie sailed for Skibo castle leaving behind him a memorandum for John A. Potter, superintendent of the Homestead works, "to roll a large set of plates ahead, which can be finished should the works be stopped for a time."

Frick wrote Pinkerton on the 25th of June: "We will want 300 guards for service at our Homestead mills against interference with our plan to start operations July sixth.."

Carnegie told about it later: "While in Scotland I received the following cable from the officers of the union of our workmen: 'Kind master, tell us what you wish us to do, and we shall do it for you..' This was most touching, but alas, too late."

Too late, the cable was delayed in reaching him. Carnegie was not at Skibo, was at Loch Rannock, Perthshire, 35 miles from a railroad station or a telegraph office.

5

Too late. For six days the men had tried desperately to get in touch with him.

Henry Phipps told about it later: "We his partners were of the opinion that the welfare of the company required he should not be in this country at this time. We knew of his extreme disposition to always grant the demands of labor, and all rejoiced we were permitted to manage the affair in our own way."

A bad affair.. July sixth a bad day in Homestead.. an all-day battle, with dynamite and dead men. The Pinkerton brigade was run out of town between lines of slugging.

Berkmann told about it later: "Carnegie selected Frick, bloody Frick of the coke regions, to carry the program into execution. Must the oppressed forever submit? Human life is indeed sacred, but to remove a tyrant is the giving of life and opportunity to an oppressed people.. On and on rushes the engine.. 'Pittsburgh! Pittsburgh!' the harsh cry of the conductor startles me."

Major General Snowden encamped at Homestead with 8000 guardsmen. "We propose to manage our own business as we think proper and right," said Frick.

Even if it calls 8000 guardsmen away from *their* own business.

Berkmann had more to tell: "I find myself facing a blackbearded figure at a table in the back of the room. 'Frick,' I begin. The look of terror on his face strikes me speechless. I aim at his head. He averts his face. The high-ceilinged room reverberates. I hear a sharp piercing cry and see Frick on his knees, his head against the arm of his chair. 'Dead?' I wonder. I must make sure. I crawl in the direction of the voice, dragging struggling men with me— get the dagger from my pocket—repeatedly strike with it—my

6

arms are pulled and twisted and I am lifted bodily. My eyes meet Frick's. He stands in front of me, supported. His face is ashen grey; the black beard is streaked with red, blood is oozing from his neck. A strange feeling as of shame comes over me; but the next moment I am filled with anger at this sentiment so unworthy of a revolutionist."

Colonel Harvey told about it later (everyone told about it but Frick): "The first bullet passed through the neck near the base of the skull and down between the shoulders; the second bullet passed through the right side of the neck. Mr Frick, in a low voice. .'Don't kill him—let the law take its course; but raise his head and let me see his face. .' The Sheriff, following the direction indicated by Mr Frick's index finger, saw that Berkmann had a capsule between his teeth. 'Remove that capsule.' It contained fulminate of mercury,* enough to blow all in the room to bits."

Surgeons probed for the bullets. Frick refused ether. "Without it I can help more in locating them," he said. He completed the day's work propped at his desk.

In the ambulance to his home in Homewood that evening, he dictated these words for the newspapers: "I do not think I shall die; but whether I do or not, the company will pursue the same policy and it will win."

He did not die; but his baby boy, Henry Clay Frick junior, born the day of the Homestead battle, died twenty-eight days later.

August fifth Frick walked alone across his lawn, stepped upon an open trolley car, entered his office at the stroke of eight, and

* *The capsule of fulminate of mercury mentioned by Col Harvey and Winkler does not appear in Berkmann's detailed account. I had arranged the cadences of my page before I noticed the discrepancy.*

rang for the morning's mail. "If an honest American cannot live in his own home without a bodyguard, it is time to quit," he told the reporters.

Out at Homestead it kept on, about the worst affair ever for strikers and their wives and children.

Ben Butler wanted Carnegie extradited for murder.

General Grosvenor called him the arch-sneak of this age.

A London paper said: "Here we have this Scotch-Yankee plutocrat meandering through Scotland in a four-in-hand opening public libraries, while the wretched workmen who supply him with ways and means for his self-glorification are starving in Pittsburgh."

A St Louis paper said:"Say what you will of Frick, he is a brave man. Say what you will of Carnegie, he is a coward. And gods and men hate cowards."

But Gladstone wrote Carnegie:". .simply to say. .that no one who knows you will be prompted by unfortunate occurrences across the water of which manifestly we cannot know the exact merits, to qualify in the slightest degree either his confidence in your generous views or his admiration of the great and good work you have done. Wealth is at present like a monster threatening to swallow up the moral life of man—you, by precept and example, have been teaching him to disgorge. .Very faithfully yours. ."

Carnegie and President Harrison had been friends, but after Homestead could a Republican win? Carnegie cut his $50,000 campaign subscription to $10,000.

8

Frick wrote Carnegie November ninth, "I am very sorry for President Harrison, but I cannot see that our interests are going to be affected."

Carnegie wrote Frick the same day: "Cleveland landslide! Well! People will now think Protected Mfgrs. will be attended to, and quit agitating. Cleveland is a pretty good fellow.. Off for Venice to-morrow."

Frick cabled Carnegie November 21st: "Strike declared off yesterday. Our victory is now complete and most gratifying."

The profits of the Company would be only $300,000 under the $4,300,000 earned the previous year.

Carnegie cabled back: "Life worth living again.. The first happy morning since July.. Surprising how pretty Italia." But he wrote Frick from Rome: "Think I'm about ten years older. Europe has rung with Homestead, Homestead, until we are all sick of the name; but it is all over now. Ever your pard, A.C."

Greed and human kindness fought each other so in Carnegie that he almost got a neurosis out of it. He fought it off as he ran by throwing gifts behind him to the Shade that followed.

Berkmann wrote: "I had attempted the life of a great magnate.. They took advantage of my refusal to be legally represented. If I had seven years, I might try. I might live a year or two, anyway. But twenty-two years!"

He underestimated his vitality.

* * *

The winter that year was a bad winter. My father took the pews

9

out of the old church on Liberty street so that more people could sleep there. I can't remember that he did much that winter except feed men, women and children. He had to hurry about, getting the money to pay for the food. He had to get it from those who had it, of course. He had to ask them for it.

One night something wakened me. I ran into the kitchen; my mother was washing blood off my father's face. That evening Mr Hamilton had driven my father over to Allegheny to see a rich man. On the way home as they came up Liberty avenue, a drunken fellow with a smart team of black horses made for them, zigzagging from one side of the street to the other. "We were thrown from the buggy.. Mr Hamilton is all right. I landed on my nose by the mare's hoofs. She stood still, she didn't kick. I'm all right, too."

This scene, woven into the other strands at the beginning of me,
lying hidden below nearly all I think and do,
along with Homestead, along with Carnegie, Frick, Berkmann:
Liberty avenue grows into a thoroughfare six times the breadth
        of other thoroughfares—
a red moon lights it from the end by the river;
the pavement is smooth, is black as death—
the buildings go up six times as high as other buildings—
the white mare pulls the buggy this way and that, fights
        her lonely duel—
there is no one on the sidewalks, not a lighted window
        in the skyscrapers—
the white mare cannot escape the black horses; they crash.
But she stands steady; my father gets only a bloody nose.

And along with this,
and along with Homestead, and Carnegie, Frick, and Berkmann,
10

another strand of childhood—the enhalo'd image
     of a full dinner pail—
what later year, what Pittsburgh street, I cannot now recall;
but the President of the United States, Major William McKinley
standing up in a barouche in a great crowd,
and I on my father's shoulder, seeing close to me
the beautiful calm face of McKinley, the all-powerful
     all-beneficent
beautiful calm face of government and business united,
promising us food. Never again
was a face to sink so deep into my life as his face,
uniting and solving the duality of the world.

* * *

Berkmann found life in prison as absorbing as out of it.

A man with smoked glasses said to him:"Didn't you come from
New York? Then, how could the strike concern you? You must
have had a personal grudge against Frick."

A Homestead striker he expected sympathy from, said: "Of
course Frick deserved to die. He is a murderer. But the mill-
workers will have nothing to do with anarchists. What did you
want to kill him for, anyway? You don't belong to the Home-
stead men; it was none of your business."

An unknown person sent him a dollar bill and a brief note:"I am
not an anarchist, but I wish you well. My sympathy is with the
man, however, not with the act. I cannot justify your attempt.
Life, human life, is sacred. None has the right to take what he
cannot give."

Had Berkmann killed Frick, we should not have seen Frick in
action against Carnegie (what we needed to see also), only in

11

action against strikers, against anarchists. We should not have seen Frick the striker, striking because he thought Carnegie had treated *him* unjustly, the same virile resentment in Frick as in the Homestead men.

1899 added these colors to our picture of Frick, a man like Berkmann, holding to what he considered justice, stopped by nothing. Had Berkmann killed him he could not have written these words in a minute of the Carnegie Steel Co., November 2nd, and read them calmly to the directors (who were not calm): "I learn that Mr Carnegie, while here, stated that I showed cowardice in not bringing up the question of coke as between Steel and Coke companies.." and added, "Why was Mr Carnegie not manly enough to say to my face what he said behind my back? He must apologise."

Whatever one may think of the dismayed directors or the infuriated Laird of Skibo or the ejecture proceedings which followed, one wonders whether a nation can develop without the men who at each stage of their own development stand up for what they consider justice—even the tough ones who go through shooting, stabbing, strikes, and the cabals of hostile barons.

What matter whether Frick was right, so long as he was Frick? What matter whether the Homestead men were right; what matter whether *you* were right, Berkmann? The waves smash against the rocks, boulder thunders upon boulder. Granite men grind one another, leaving their clean sand to floor the ocean.

The alternative would be for the republic to breed up a race of men who could work together without growing violent: men more interested in getting somewhere than in having their own way.

12

Berkmann, the strikers, Frick and Phipps and the other barons, all believed they were right, and were ready to take punishment for what they believed. And so they were putting themselves in position to learn, whether they learned or not.

The Homestead strikers were Americans; many of them had been boys on farms near Pittsburgh like Frick himself. There was no difference of kind between Frick and the strikers. After Homestead, labor tended to be foreign labor and more or less a state of peonage. The gap between owners and workers became a thing to torture the conscience. It got so bad that R.B.Mellon told a senate committee you couldn't run a coal mine without machine guns.

The Homestead strike was bad, but its results have been horrible. Yet how is one to talk it over quietly with people ready to die (or to kill others) for what they believe?

At the time only Carnegie seemed more complicated. There was clearly a doubt in Carnegie. He concerns us more than people who are ready to die (or to kill others) for what they believe. Maybe culture or religion had begun to break him down.

Like Berkmann, Carnegie had the gift of gab; they both describe their mothers. Carnegie says: "Mother had cooked and served her boys, washed their clothes and mended them, made their beds, cleaned their home.. There was nothing that heroine didn't do in the struggle we were making for elbow room in the western world.. But we could not escape the inevitable servant girl. One came and others followed, and with these came also the destruction of much of that genuine family happiness that flows from exclusiveness.."

Carnegie promised his mother never to marry while she lived. He did not want his mother worn out contending with a daughter-in-law. He kept his word, did not marry till he was fifty-two.

Berkmann says:"I resented my mother's right to inflict physical punishment on the servants.'You have no right to strike the girl. . She is as good as you.' Mother's long slender fingers grasp the heavy ladle, and the next instant a sharp pain pierces my left hand. Her arm remains motionless, her gaze directed to the spreading blood stain on the table cloth. Without a word I pick up the heavy salt cellar and fling it against the French mirror. At the crash of the glass my mother opens her eyes. I rise and leave the house."

Even as a boy, Mr Carnegie, this comrade of yours and mine had to smash something; but like you, he loved his mother too much to smash *her*, and so the looking glass got it.

As usual in such cases, the looking glass got it; what was reflected in the looking glass got it.

Homestead, Loch Rannock. . .

The arch-sneak of the age? It looks as though you were, Mr Carnegie—but sneaking from the arch-question of your age. Berkmann and Frick, being less adult, thought they had the right answer to the arch-question, or to any question. They did not need to sneak, they could be brave.

The arch-question bothered you a good deal. It kept you in hot water with yourself most of your later life. You wrote pamphlets about it and mailed one to Grover Cleveland, to find out what he thought (because you knew he was no fool), and he wrote back: *Executive Mansion, Washington, D.C.*— "Dear Mr Carnegie:. . You state the rule which must underlie any effective remedy, when you say:'You must capture and keep the heart of the original and supremely able man before his brain can do its

14

best'—but I am sure your own experience justifies you in further saying:'You must capture and keep the heart of any *working man* before his *hands* will do their best..''

Mr Carnegie, President Cleveland asked you the question we are asking you to-day, with what end in view is a man's heart to be won?

A leaf of paper flutters down to us, do you recall it, a private memorandum of yours: December 1868, St Nicholas Hotel, New York–"Thirty-three. At 35 will have an income of $50,000 per annum: beyond this never earn. The amassing of wealth is one of the worst species of idolatry.. no idol is more debasing.. Resign business at 35, settle in Oxford, get a thorough education, make the acquaintance of literary men.. To continue to make money must degrade me beyond hope of recovery.. Settle then in London, purchase a controlling interest in some live review, taking part in public matters, especially those concerned with education and improvement of the poorer classes.."

There by Loch Rannock did you regret the growth of the company, the always increasing cry for profits?

A time had been when you went to the yards yourself and talked their grievances over with the men. The stool of business has three legs, you used to say—labor, capital, management— and the greatest of these is management.

The great new word management, seed for the future: were you not the first to isolate this health-giving germ?

Were not those days by the loch, black days in your soul? Did you imagine in any nightmare how it might work out if management and labor combined against ownership?

These Pittsburgh men and boys working your mills,
walking your streets, these delicate living columns
caught in the black and widening web of your iron,
the masculine smouldering of their lives stranger
in the mesh of steel, in the webbed aluminum,
always to be stranger, more gleaming, than skein of metal;
whether magnesium, or an undreamt metal, comes,
always with their full healthy bloom of life,
their sleepy bliss, their painful urgent angers,
to be more complicated, more attractive
to thought, than any world thought can erect
under a spectral whisper which forgets
the quick for the dead. Time brings forth ages like ours
when all things move fast; and it is better
to have all things move fast, better at least
for those who follow you, and follow us.
Yes, it is better; it will be shown to be better.

This obscure hurt which never gives us peace..
We can explain why it is not our fault,
but it remains our fault.
We can distract ourselves, but the hurt is there,
our slow undoing through our sympathies:
the slow coming to birth within our living
body, of the new body made of ours.
Yet in the business of childbirth, certainly,
all effort bends on the delivery
of that new body to the world in all
its wholeness: the mother out of whom new life
is coming, we the mother, we scream, we faint,
we die perhaps, are not aware of what we do
or how disturbing our outcries may be
to the public, the public order, the prevailing,
the preferred, the accustomed—

                              When it is born
    the new being will answer to all that,
    is it not so?

Some disturbances are cosmic, with vibrations in every mind.
Whitman had vibrated: "I do not give a little charity. When I
give, I give myself."

Schopenhauer too had vibrated: "The good man wants the least
difference possible made between himself and others."

You yourself, Mr Carnegie: "The amassing of wealth is one of
the worst species of idolatry."

If one might see into you seated there by Loch Rannock, 35
miles from a telegraph office, might one not study in you a cos-
mic storm, reflected in miniature: the idea of, the necessity of,
the disappearance of the individual?

Who can say? You were no ordinary person, but it all seems
long ago.

STEPHEN FOSTER
1894

Another Pittsburgher, another life, another way of life: thirtieth anniversary of Stephen Foster's death, January 13, 1894.

"No other single individual," wrote Milligan, "produced so many of those songs..called folk-songs.. All things must have a beginning..every folk-song is first born in the heart of some one person, whose spirit is so finely attuned to the inward struggle which is the history of the soul of man, that when he seeks for his self-expression, he at the same time gives voice to that 'vast multitude who die and give no sign'.."

A life "sadly out of harmony with its environment"; and yet, "if I make the songs of a people," I care not.

The boy was born on a fourth of July—not the fourth of Gettysburg and Vicksburg, nor the fourth of Santiago, but the fourth of 1826 when Jefferson died at high noon and Adams at sunset.

Harmony, Pa., May 4, 1832: Mrs Foster to her son William: " ...the little children go to school with quite as happy faces as though the world had no thorns in it, and I confess there would be but few if we would all follow the scriptures, in which we would be made strong.. Stephen has a drum and marches about after the old way with a feather in his hat and a girdle round his waist, whistling *Auld Lang Syne*.. There still remains something perfectly original about him."

Something perfectly original, which was to give him trouble when he went to school and afterwards.

Youngstown, January 14, 1837: "dear Father: I wish you to send me a commic songster for you promised to. If I had my pensyl I could rule my paper or if I had the money to buy black ink—but if I had my whistle I w'd be so taken with it I do not think I w'd write a tall..Stephen."

His " 'ittle pizano" was his sister's guitar. "Not until twenty years later was the first upright piano brought across the mountains."

Senator Kingsbury of Minnesota: "Stephen and I often played truant together, going barefoot, gathering wild strawberries by shady streams. It shocked me to see him cast away his fine hose when spoiled by perspiration or muddy water.. His execution on the flute was the genius of melody."

Youngstown, August 7, 1840: Mrs Foster to her son William: "..as to Stephen, I leave everything regarding the future to your own judgment, West Point or the Navy, I have no choice; you are not only his Brother, but his Father; and I trust all his feelings will ascend to you as his Patron.."

"Dear William, there is a good fire place in my room and if you will just say the word I will have a fire in it at nights and learn something. Don't forget my waistcoat at the tailor's. Your affectionate brother, Stephen."

"..people liked to hear the boy sing Zip Coon and Longtail Blue..but such music as he came in contact with was so associated with idleness and dissipation as to be regarded at best only as an amiable weakness."

And the boy himself began to write songs. He wrote one about a good time coming:

20

"Little children shall not toil under or above the soil,
But shall play in healthful fields,
In the good time coming.."
Peters and Field published it in Cincinnati in 1846.

And he attended a Pittsburgh theatre on Fifth Street, "an un-pretentious structure rudely built of boards but sufficient to secure the comfort of the few who dared to face the consequences and lend their patronage to an establishment under the ban of the Scotch-Irish Calvinists." (Nevin)

And he wrote more songs, and kept on writing songs: "*Nelly Bly, Nelly was a Lady, Dolcy Jones, etc. Aethiopian Melodies by the Author of Uncle Ned and O Susanna.* Firth, Pond & Co., New York 1850."

So that at twenty-three he had set his country singing.

Allegheny City, June 21, 1853, sister Henrietta to brother Morrison: "How sorry I feel for poor Stephy, though when I read your letter I was not at all surprised at the news in regard to him and——(name scratched out). Last winter I felt convinced ——(three lines scratched out, ending in the word "mistake").. May God lead him in the ways of peace, fill his heart with that love which alone is satisfying."

Stephen had left home, stayed in various places, finally settled in New York, where he wrote fourteen more songs, among them *Sewanee River.* "Aside from one or two national airs born out of great historical crises, probably the most widely known song ever written... translated into every language, sung by millions.. in some subtle and instinctive way it expresses the homesick yearning over the past and far away which is the common emotional heritage of the race.." (Milligan)

21

Pittsburgh, March 3, 1854: brother Dunning to brother William: "Have you heard anything from Stephen lately? It is a subject of much anxiety to me; notwithstanding his foolish and unaccountable course, I hope he will continue to make a comfortable living for himself.."

"The mother of the celebrated song writer" died in January, 1855. In the obituaries Stephen's name is mentioned before that of his father, twice mayor of Allegheny City, or that of his brother, builder of the Pennsylvania Railroad.

"Herz, Sivori, Ole Bull and Thalberg were ready to approve his genius, and chose his melodies about which to weave their witcheries."

And no one knows much more about Stephen except when he came to die.

"N.Y. City, January 12, 1864, Morrison Foster, Esq., Your brother Stephen is lying in Bellevue Hospital..very sick.. He desires me to ask you to send him some pecuniary assistance.. If possible he would like to see you in person..George Cooper."

Cleveland, January 14, 1864 (by telegraph from New York): "To Morrison Foster, Stephen is dead. Come on. George Cooper."

And George Cooper's account was: "I received a message saying my friend had met with an accident.. I dressed hurriedly and went to 15 Bowery..found him lying on the floor in the hall, blood oozing from a cut in his throat and with a bad bruise on his forehead.. Steve never wore night clothes..lay there naked suffering horribly.. The doctor arrived..started to sew up Steve's throat with black thread. 'Haven't you any white

22

thread?' I asked, and he said 'no'.. I decided the doctor was not much good.. went downstairs and got Steve a big drink of rum, which seemed to help him.. We put his clothes on him and took him to the hospital.. He seemed terribly weak and his eyelids kept fluttering.. I went back to the hospital to see him next day.. He said nothing had been done for him, and he couldn't eat the food.. Next day they said, 'Your friend is dead.' Steve's body had been sent down to the morgue. There was an old man sitting there smoking a pipe. I told him what I wanted and he said, 'Go look for him.' I went around peering into the coffins until I found Steve's body.. Next day, his brother Morrison and Steve's widow arrived."

"Bellevue Hospital, Ward 11, Stephen Foster, Died Jan 13th: Coat, pants, vest, hat, shoes, overcoat Jan 10th 1864. Rec'd of Mr Foster ten shillings charge for Stephen C. Foster while in hospital. Wm. E. White, warden."

Died and went naked into the next world, as all men must.

"There was a tendency of habit grown insidiously upon him.. against which, as no one better than this writer knows" (this writer being Nevin) "he wrestled with earnestness indescribable."

And Morrison Foster, thus to an editor:".. the public knew not *him*, but only *of* him, his poetry and music being the only visible sign that such a person really existed at all..reference to certain peculiarities is not only out of place but a cruel tearing open of wounds, which the grave should close forever."

And yet, Morrison Foster, your brother being in a certain sense not only Pittsburgh's greatest but America's.. Coat, pants, vest, these do not concern us, but what of the wounds and what caused them?

23

"Who can say what would have been the sum of Franz Schubert's achievements had he been born in Pittsburgh in 1826?"

What in fact was the sum of anybody's achievements who couldn't be a farmer or a manufacturer or a trader or a politician or a doctor or a lawyer—couldn't help materially in the young city's life?

What is the sum of their achievements to-day, these unfortunates?

* * *

Up from his blood and entrails through years of blackness
came the ghosts. He did not give a little charity,
gave himself, rendered back to us the old ghosts,
kept himself a gateway for songs
of homelessness, despair and tears,
agonies of a foundling crying for the harmony
out of which he was born.

Thirty-eight years it took his world to kill him,
the fragile masculine nature fighting
not only the enemies outside him, but those inside,
fear, and a sense of guilt—
his love for his good mother, whose love of him
wavered at his gift, seeing the gift as a hindrance
to a useful life ending in comfort and money—
his love for his sister,
who thought the love of God would work out better
for Stephen than a human love,
putting this confusion between the Door
and the Temple the Door opens into—
and the magnificent brother, builder of the P.R.R.—
and the father, twice mayor of Allegheny City—
and the other brothers, fine fellows

24

marching along content in the regiment,
Stephen at their side, wistful, out of step,
needing support in a nature that amounted to rebellion,
finding support in no one near him where it might count,
but always vague—his country's love of his songs
being like a surf that breaks a long distance off.
Doubtless real women lived then, as ever,
who would have seen him as a gateway for the ghosts,
freed his limbs and heart, intoxicated him and not with whiskey
but he did not find such women, looked for them no doubt,
but did not find them. And so there was a habit
grown insidiously upon him—
so that he would not need to ask himself if it was right
to listen to the murmur of blood and bone within him,
to try to catch what he could of a melody
very strange and disturbing, brain-throttled, fear-stifled,
yet going all through him.

"Mine, O thou lord of life, send my roots rain."

Orange leaf of a moon, holding on to the horizon,
what do you see in the last hours of night?

If you know what dreaming means,
                    says one of Strauss's love songs,
If you knew it, you would come to me.
                    But when you do not come
not you, nor I, more than a sparrow or than twigs in twilight
shall leave on earth a token of our presence.
"If I had my pensyl I could rule my paper
but if I had my whistle I w'd be so taken with it
I do not think I w'd write a tall."

I w'd only whistle, all day long I w'd whistle;

but if I were still unhappy and my heart ached—
                          then, as it is writ in Proverbs,
"Give strong drink unto him that is ready to perish,
and wine unto those that be of heavy hearts;
let him drink and forget his poverty,
and remember his misery no more."

West Point or the Navy, his mother had no choice;
but cursed with a something perfectly original
he pursued his foolish and unaccountable course,
this our beloved, O Pittsburghers,
till he died and went naked into the next world
                          as all men must,
along with Carnegie, Frick, Henry Phipps,
                          Gladstone, Robert A. Pinkerton,
                          and Grover Cleveland—

the next world where, it is said, the soul of a man matters.

This our beloved . .
                          the day he died
" . . horrors, portioned to a giant nerve,
Oft made Hyperion ache."

JOHN BRASHEAR
1894

Still another Pittsburgher, still another life, still another way of life.

This year, 1894, John Brashear completed the spectrograph for Lick Observatory.

"It is doubtful whether any other ever contained prisms more perfect," says Scaife. "It..rendered possible a new and revolutionary attack on the stars."

Brashear had grown up in the mill valleys and when he was old enough he got a job in the mills, like the other boys.

He used to sit on the hill at night, looking at the stars for hours. He liked the goblin forges along the river, but the stars fascinated him.

When he married he built his house with his own hands, and cut a hole in the roof for a telescope.

He began to use his spare time making lenses for telescopes, and his wife helped him. She tended the fires while he was at the mills, and towards evening saw that everything was ready. She watched for him coming up the hill, and they had supper and afterwards went to work on the lenses.

"Phoebe never fails me," he used to say. It was that kind of marriage.

There was a moment when he thought it might be better to be a preacher than to make lenses. The minister was to be away one Sunday, and Brashear was asked to take the pulpit. He spoke on the first four verses of Genesis, viewing creation from the scientific side. The minister as it happened had not gone away after all; he was there, and heard what Brashear said. When the service was over, he said to the young man: "Your talk was interesting, but I do not think a knowledge of creation is necessary to the believer or the seeker after truth; for the Bible teaches us, if we believe, we shall be saved, and if we believe not, we shall be damned, and this is the sum and substance of the whole matter."

"One of the most painful episodes of my life," said Brashear long after. "Those cruel words still ring in my ears."

Phoebe and he went back to making lenses so people could see the stars better.

Brashear was the kind of young man whom a man like William Thaw would notice and be interested in. (There had been a Pittsburgh before the one I write of, with strong and good men in it.)

Now and then a man stands before the stars as he stands before his family or his fellow men or his enemies, with the circle of his integrity drawn, and all his ghosts inside him, working for him and not against him.

Brashear's lenses went all over the world, and they were always better than was expected.

He and his wife saw the traffic wars, saw the long steel railroads turn and rend each other; they saw the other wars, the riots of '73, Homestead, McKees' Rocks, the endless war of city graft, the Civil War, the Spanish War. He lived on after her, and saw the World War.

It is not easy to make a fine lens. The trouble is to obtain discs of the requisite size, free from striae, from inequalities of the density specified, from hygroscopic and other defects—some of which can be discovered only after the glass is polished.

In 1915 he wrote to a friend:".. one of the things that has brought much happiness to me is that I have been able to carry out my lifelong design to have a department of astronomy free to the people.."

When he died he left a note:"If my dear friend of many years, Dr. A. J. Bonsall, who conducted the services of my dear companion, will also conduct the services at my obsequies, I will be very content, for he knows I have no love for those services in which the Great Creator is mentioned as a god of vengeance.."

..A.J.Bonsall—like Brashear himself a light-house, a compass, a spring in the desert..

It is not easy to make a fine lens. It took Brashear himself seventeen years to make the 30-inch object glass for the Thaw Memorial.

He lies with his wife in the New Allegheny Observatory, with an epitaph they had agreed on together:

> Phoebe S. Brashear   1843-1910
> *We have loved the stars too fondly*
> *To be fearful of the night.*
> John A. Brashear   1840-1920

* * *

Frick was sure God was with him.

So was Berkmann.

Reality almost gave Carnegie a neurosis.

Carnegie at 33 saw that the amassing of money was bad for a
man. But he could not stop amassing it. He spent time working
out a gospel of wealth to justify himself.

Brashear walked through Pittsburgh like a visitor from the Is-
lands of the Blest.

Maybe Brashear had a sixth sense, maybe he was reborn.

Some people are not afraid things can overpower them.
Some people can accept things without forcing their will upon
them.

Could you imagine Brashear thinking that God was on his side?
About as far as you could go would be that he hoped he was on
God's side.

Maybe if we keep on knifing one another we will get sick of it
finally. When a man sickens of violence and self-assertion, some-
times a spirit flows into him the way the ocean flows into an
inlet.

> One looks into the great vault above, at midnight,
> and sees the stars—recognizes some, notes that as ever
> they follow their orbits; that Law rules their bright travels.
> One gazes
> into the midnight of a fellow human being, and sees the stars,
> or does not see the stars,

or sees them strayed from their orbits: and has the same
                    sensation of Law,
and a more intimate and terrible knowledge of its beauty,
                    because of the changes
and the destructions in a human being who will not or can not
                    or dare not
abide by the Law of his nature and the law of the species.

"I love to love, and loving to love search something to love.."
In St Augustine the needle quivered there most of the time,
                    as it does in us.
St Augustine found something to love, and so may we.

And there is Handel's aria, "When thou appearest, all will be
                    restored to me!"

M

en in action are the poet's proper theme;
statistics are the footprints of men in action,
"thick statistical volumes, the modern tragic dramas."

1865	Kloman Phipps	Capital	$150,000
1873	Carnegie McCandless Co.	"	700,000
1874	Edgar Thompson Steel Co.	"	1,000,000
1881	Carnegie Bros. & Co.	"	5,000,000
1892	Carnegie Steel Co., Ltd.	"	25,000,000
1901	United States Steel Corporation	"	1,403,000,000

And so Carnegie retired from business with four hundred million dollars. March 12th he wrote from New York: "I make this first use of surplus wealth, four millions of first mortgage bonds.., as an acknowledgment of the deep debt which I owe the workmen who have contributed so greatly to my success.."

And Harry F. Rose, roller;)
John Bell, Jr., blacksmith;)
J. A. Horton, timekeeper;)
Walter Grieg, foreman;)
Harry Cusack, yardmaster,) wrote back to Carnegie from Munhall, Pa.,—".. of the many channels through which you have sought to do good, we believe that the Andrew Carnegie Relief Fund stands first. We have personal knowledge of cares lightened and of hope and strength renewed in homes where human prospects seemed dark and discouraging.. Respectfully.."

Carnegie kept on giving away his money as fast as he could.

Of another minor gift, half a million sterling in bonds bearing five percent, he wrote:"It seems poetic justice that the grandson of Thomas Morrison, radical leader in his day,..that above all the son of my sainted father and my most heroic mother, should arise and dispossess the lairds, should become the agent for conveying the glen and the park to the people of Dunfermline forever..to bring into the monotonous lives of the toiling masses of Dunfermline more of sweetness and light, to give to them, especially to the young, some charm, some happiness, some elevating conditions of life, which residence elsewhere would have denied.."

..residence in Homestead, for example..

And yet this was no ordinary man, this Carnegie.

No one is ordinary who tries to get beyond a selfish joy in his power to an unselfish use of it.

And in "The Gospel of Wealth," written to quiet the inward doubt, he continues:"When visiting the Sioux, I was led to the wigwam of their chief. It was like the others in external appearance, and even within the difference was trifling. The contrast between the palace of the millionaire and the cottage of the laborer with us to-day, measures the change which has come with civilisation..a change not to be deplored, but welcomed as highly beneficial.. The problem of our age is the problem of the proper administration of wealth, that the ties of brotherhood may still bind together the rich and the poor in harmonoius relationship.. It is the duty of the millionaire to increase his revenues.. The struggle for more is completely freed from selfishness or ambitious taint and becomes a noble pursuit..he labors not for self, but for others; not to hoard, but to spend.."

That is, you take money from people and then give it back to them, and call it a life.

Whether you benefit others by being generous is a question. It is no question that you benefit yourself, and owe others gratitude for the chance of self-improvement.

No doubt eternity demands full restitution, and Carnegie knew it.

Some natures cannot force the tire to submit to the hub in a single life time. We all need more than one life time.

When he died at Lenox in 1919, Carnegie had succeeded in giving away $350,695,650.10 of the four hundred million. He had his epitaph ready: "Here lies a man who knew how to enlist in his services better men than himself." In the end his answer to the arch-question of the age was no answer, was only fooling.

Some people read about Carnegie and called him a great man.

Others read about Carnegie and became frantic.

He was even summoned before a congressional committee and asked whether his enormous gifts did not endanger democratic institutions.

Some people became anarchists reading about Carnegie.

Others saw him as a portent. They went back and read our history to find out how he fitted into it.

Our history is in three stages. Alexis de Tocqueville described the first stage when he told about staying overnight in 1838 at the home of a planter in western Pennsylvania: "In democratic countries, the majority of the people do not clearly see what they have to gain by revolution, but they continually and in a thousand ways feel what they might lose by one.. In no country is the love of property more active and more anxious than in the United States.."

The second stage was described in words attributed to Lincoln: "As a result of the war, corporations have been enthroned..and the money power of the country will endeavor to prolong its reign..until all wealth is aggregated in a few hands.. I feel more anxiety for the safety of my country than ever before, even in the midst of war."

The third stage still continues.

Judge Grosscup described it in McClure's Magazine in 1905: "The soul of republican America is the opportunity and encouragement given to each to build up, by his own efforts, and for himself and those dependent on him, some measure of dominion and independence all his own.. In (those words) is comprised the civil history of the Anglo-Saxon race.. The loss that republican America now confronts is the loss of individual hope and prospect.."

The Judge said we had better find a way to make this new form of property called corporations, a "workable agent for putting the people back into the proprietorship of the country's industries." He called this next step "re-people-ising industry."

1901   United States Steel Corporation   Capital $1,403,450,000

Which monster growth, along with others like it, did not go un-

marked but was observed narrowly by thousands the world over.
Monster growths of business, tremendous and terrible music in
the newspapers, in the thoughts of men.

Some men, driven by a haste cosmic and not human,
built furiously, like titans or like idiots, a new world.

Sometimes a man thinks he is doing something for himself
when the morning stars know better.

But no longer (if ever the heart believed it)
can the Napoleon-man be thought the great man.
Our memories, though sown of blood and death,
are humid with the roots of a fresh life.
The marrow of the race remains as always:
it shapes its thought, disseminates its meaning
wherever the sun goes, lends magnetism
to those who show how deadening at the last
the ego is, bent upon ego-business.
Henceforth we search success elsewhere, the life-thought
living us as it may: the ungenerous roles
are there to play, but who will care to play them
when roles more virile, shrewder purposes
to tempt the spirit, open up about us—
novel, more hazardous, more interesting,
employing all of a man, making him more
the man?
             It grows too clear how personal life
destroys its pattern; understanding this,
delight throbs in our blood, and in the mind
a new hope blooms, up from the ageless marrow
which rules our life and which we cannot rule.

The great man of the future fights for life

on the widest fronts we know, the front of the inward,
the front of the outward.
                              The great man fights
for his life and for ours, and for the health
of the relationships of men.
                              He knows
that what goes to and fro between the stars,
between the sea and land, goes to and fro
between himself and all.
                              He tries to blaze
the trail for us to follow, by accepting
the human ties of his life—and out of love,
not fear or duty: the pathway of the future
is the path of interweaving so accepted:
he feels the mysterious urging of his marrow
and he obeys, because he is the great man.

MRS SOFFEL
1902

Friday, January 31, 1902
the Biddle brothers, Jack and Ed, escaped
from murderers' row in the Allegheny County jail,
the jail of Richardson romanesque which makes downtown
Pittsburgh even to the eye baronial, and brings back
the dark strongholds and the dark sieges of feudalism
when likewise a baron was a baron.
                              The boys escaped
from that keep which never had been expected
to yield up victim. The warden's wife had seen
prisoners year in, year out; they meant nothing to her.
But the day came when the robber brothers were arrested:
with another robber, named Dorman, they had broken
into a store, and the night watchman was found slain,
and Dorman turned state's evidence, and swore
that the Biddles killed him. Mrs Soffel, like others,
believed that Dorman lied. The brothers drew
her pity—in particular Ed, a quiet
soft-spoken enigmatic fellow. Through her friends
she petitioned the governor for mercy; but, it is plain,
expected him to show none, and the noose came nearer
hourly. And so she read the Bible aloud
to the Biddles, and they sawed through the bars of the cell.
"With your love I can start over," Ed told her,
and she believed him. She had seen many prisoners,
but she believed Ed; her heart had given her orders.
Her face in the newspaper-pictures had a look
a good deal at variance with down-town Pittsburgh
and the brownstone jail.

39

The boys escaped from that keep
which never gave up its victims, and Mrs Soffel
went with them. At the bitter moment of sacrifice
it may be that she failed; yet through her failure
Pittsburgh gained hero as well heroine—for Ed
could not let her believe that they had used her selfishly,
and they went away together, not as they had planned,
separately, to meet later. The remainder of that night
they stayed on Plush Way, in the evil first ward
of Allegheny, and in the intense cold of the morning
took the Perry Highway towards Butler, a road
through fog-filled glens of winter, walking along
leisurely in the snow, observing the world they would soon
be leaving, and saying a few things we can imagine
about winter cold, and another cold, and the world
they would soon be leaving.

                            And one asks oneself why Jack
did not desert the lovers and save himself,
what Jack considered of greater price than life.

Growing tired of walking, they stole a horse and a sleigh
and went on. At twilight the second day, near Prospect,
detectives were hiding behind the crest of a hill.
"Spread out, and mind you keep cool," said McGovern—they
were nervous, and so was the whole countryside:
yet, and clearly by agreement, at the first shot
Mrs Soffel shot herself (through the breast,
missing the heart), Jack shot himself (through the mouth,
but had eight other bullets in him when they counted),
and Ed, though he took pot shots at the officers,
was shot only once, and that was the death bullet
he gave himself.

                    Later, when Mrs Soffel
opened her eyes in the Butler jail, they told her

the boys were dead, and she said, "I am alone now."
It was no more than the truth. At the begrimed jail
in the heart of the town of Butler they charged admission
to see the bodies of the boys (an event of this kind
being a plain windfall to them, as indeed to us
O Pittsburghers, to-day and forever) and an attendant
kept bawling, "Gentlemen please remove their hats";
and when they closed the doors, they had to open them
again, because an aged man and a youth
had driven a long way to see the bodies, and ought to
be given a look. At Beinhauer's Funeral Parlor,
Pittsburgh, Southside, thousands of women fought
to see the dead boys, and the police had all they could do;
and a woman in deep mourning heaped evergreens
on the coffins, and it so displeased a relative of the Biddles
that he ordered the doors closed, and thus it happened
that thousands of women never saw the boys at all.

"I am alone now," and in delirium repeated,
"Don't desert me; take me with you, boys.."

"Warden Soffel was sitting in the parlor, surrounded by rela-
tives..was very nervous.. A hush pervaded the little circle and
a feeling as though there had been a death in the house. 'You
can say for me that I am heartily glad the Biddle boys were
caught. I am glad my wife was captured with them, and hope if
she lives she will be brought here and given just punishment for
her part in the crime. I hope the boys are not dead, as the
country deserves the privilege of hanging them.'"

A minister the following Sunday: "The blindness and infatua-
tion of this woman in leaving her beloved husband and helpless
little children for a gang of desperadoes, is the worst criminal act
thus far in the history of the twentieth century.."

A newspaper editorial February 3rd: "It had been expected that the men would have deserted the woman who had sacrificed everything for them and would have separated. But their gratitude was greater than they had been given credit for, and their loyalty is responsible for the fact that justice so speedily triumphed."

Reporters interviewed Mrs Soffel: "I am a bad woman. I will now go to prison if I live. I am a bad woman. I love only my children. You know there are many domestic troubles that only women can understand. I feel only for my children."

Her friends said she had been very ill and had never really recovered.

> Nothing can trick the eye of love—lovers
> knowing their identity, infinitude:
> and if the path of love be the path of death,
> it cannot frighten them—lovers knowing what is true,
> and death is a lie; knowing what really concerns them,
> and death does not.
>   The whole a manifestation
> himalayan: reminding one there are hidden forces
> to renew life, make it a sudden marvel
> of poetry, music, madness for an enslaved city
> and a love-starved people: reminding one how little
> we know of love, how well it might be to know more.
>
> My grandmother told me the story (I was fourteen,
> a good ripe age to hear it) standing
> at her churn in the old kitchen at Parker's Landing,
> as she might describe a storm that had happened near by,
> impersonally, with no moral comment, quite certain
> that here was a tale to prosper a growing lad,

quite certain, in her wisdom: the desperate blinding storm
sweeping up the valley from Pittsburgh till the winchesters
quenched it, leaving us with the memory of a heroine
who saw love and death as one, and a hero
who could make of love more than a means of escape.
Criminals all, true; yet criminals
are human beings too—how does it matter?
And there are criminals, and criminals—
but love bears witness to its mystery
wherever one can find it.
                    And of Jack Biddle
what can one say?—only, of course, that there is
Life within life, and any appearance of it
a great and shining star in a black night.

When a young fellow George Westinghouse was on a train held up near Albany because the last two cars of the train ahead of it had jumped the track, and he watched the wrecking crew pry each car back inch by inch till it could be jacked up on the rail; and he thought it was so slow, such a lot of work. He saw an easier way to do it, and he made a car-replacer and patented it and started selling it to the railroads.

One day while traveling selling his car-replacer he found a seat next to a girl and began talking with her, and she told him her name was Margaret Walker and he asked her whether he might come to Kingston and call on her. She hesitated, and he took out his notebook and wrote the names and addresses of people in Kingston who knew his family; and as soon as he reached Schenectady he asked his preacher to write a letter to Miss Walker about him. At supper that evening he told his parents he had met the girl he wanted to marry; a few months later he married her.

One day he was going to Troy and the train stopped out in the country and he got off to see what was wrong. Two freight trains had run into each other; no one was hurt but it was unsightly, boxes all over the fields. Yet the day was clear and the track straight, and there was no reason for it, and he thought about the uselessness of it. Somebody said, "They tried to stop; they saw each other, but you can't stop a freight train in a minute." "Why can't you?" asked Westinghouse.

He happened to read in a magazine how they bored the Mont

Cenis tunnel. Compressed air ought to stop a train quick, he told himself. He went to Pittsburgh, but even in Pittsburgh nobody believed you could carry compressed air under a train and set the brakes with it on the last car. Nobody except a young fellow named Baggaley whom he had stopped on the street for directions, a few minutes after leaving the station. He and Baggaley made friends; and when after six months of skeptical railroad officials, he persuaded the Panhandle to lend him an engine and four cars, it was Baggaley helped him find the money to equip the train with the new brakes.

Westinghouse and Baggaley were sure the brakes would work, but the invited officials didn't know. The train left Pittsburgh station, ran through the Grant Hill tunnel and came to the surface crossing at Fourth Avenue, and there in the middle of the tracks was a teamster and his balking horses. The train was going thirty miles an hour and Tate, the engineer, decided this was as good a time as any to try out the new brakes, and slammed them on. The officials were shaken up and frightened, but the brakes saved the teamster and his horses.

After that Westinghouse was busy selling his brakes all over the country and in Europe, and he made money and built plants.

He went on noticing people the way he had noticed Margaret Walker and Baggaley, and went on noticing things that happened, like the freight wrecks, and having ideas and inventing inventions; and he began to experiment with gas, and one day he said to his wife, "This won't be as much fun as working out the model for the air brake because I can't very well do it at home." And she said, "I think you can do it at home. I like to have you around the house, George." So he put up a derrick on the lawn of his place on Penn Avenue, and began to bore, and when the drill reached the gas field there was an explosion, and the oil

46

and sand and mud wiped out the flower beds. But Mrs Westinghouse didn't care, she was so much interested in George and his ideas about gas.

Mrs Westinghouse had ideas herself. Later on when her husband began experimenting with electricity and went into battle with Edison, supporting the alternating current against the direct current, she decided to light their summer home at Lenox with diffused electric lighting. He thought her idea premature, but to her it seemed practicable; and she was right—twenty years later illuminating engineers were still coming to Lenox to see how she had done such a good job that not a single light-bulb in the house could distress anyone.

There had been a bad time in one of the insurance companies, and the directors resigned. T.F.Ryan tried to save what he could for the widows and orphans; but before he bought control he had to be sure of a board of three prominent honest men everybody knew were honest, and he decided on Grover Cleveland and Morgan O'Brien and George Westinghouse. Westinghouse was busier than usual at the moment, but he and his wife thought he couldn't refuse anyone the use of his honesty; and so he went along with Cleveland and O'Brien and T. F. Ryan, and it ended well for the widows and orphans.

Westinghouse himself had had money trouble in 1892 and certain Pittsburgh bankers were eager to help him if he would allow them to put in a "manager"; but he couldn't see why they should put in a "manager," and said no, and went to New York and got the money he needed from Belmont. But in October 1907 he had extremely bad money trouble; it was inconvenient because he was working on the idea of a turbine, and had almost got his finger on it. This time Wall Street would not help him. Some say the Pittsburgh bankers in question had told Wall

Street to keep out of Pittsburgh; anyway, this time he was forced to apply to them, and again they were eager to help him if he would allow them to put in a "manager"; and he had to say yes.

So the bankers seized the company he had spent his life building up; but the day he failed Westinghouse said, "The company is doing more business than ever before. It will come out all right in the end. This is not pleasant, but it's only a part of our day's work."

The same afternoon he said to McFarland, "By the way, I have an idea for that turbine which will make a sensation."

Certain men know when to stop being personal, when to become impersonal. A man himself ought to amount to more than anything he does.

Some Pittsburghers thought that what Westinghouse said the day he failed was more important than any of his inventions to make people safe and comfortable.

HENRY GEORGE
1913

I. ■ The entire tax revenue for municipal purposes is derived from taxes on real estate. There are no other taxes levied by the city government on any other form of property or income. II. The municipal tax rate on buildings is fixed at one-half of the tax rate levied upon land. (Pennsylvania Laws of 1913, p. 209, No 147, for Cities of the Second Class, Pittsburgh and Scranton, Section 1, Article VI.)

And when this law was passed, Frederic C. Howe called it "the greatest single step any American city has taken in city building," and President Roosevelt wrote in the Century Magazine, "The burden of taxation should be so shifted as to put the weight upon the unearned rise in the value of the land itself."

And behind Mayor Magee and the others who fought this law through the legislature, and apart from all questions of political economy involved in it, there rises in me the image of Henry George.

And I remember his words in accepting the New York mayoralty nomination: "Years ago I came to this city from the west.. saw and recognised the shocking contrast between monstrous wealth and debasing want.. And here I made a vow from which I have never faltered, to seek and remedy, if I could, the cause that condemned little children to lead such a life as you know them to lead in the squalid districts.."

Henry George,
                    Pittsburgh is a plateau ripped up and across
by valleys, even chasms; there is a small park hard to reach,
used for botanical experiment, a long climb up to it
and you overlook a bluff and see mills and the Ohio river
between the hills below you. And you are there among the growth
they test their theories with: arenaria from the Baltic isles,
saxifrage, thyme, all kinds of small and lovely green life
for covering rocks; as well as hawthorn smelling of the salt sea,
and the grey lilac of Persia, rich as the rugs of Persia,
and black birches shaggy as goats, with the staff-vine
                    running up them
(the vine the Indians in these parts of old, ate and lived on
during hard winters when all else failed), the Oregon barberry,
Dyer's Wode with which our Saxon ancestors dyed their limbs blue
(I could see those naked blue bodies moving through the haze
                    of trees
when McCollum, the gardener, told me; and then I turned and saw
the yellow Ohio and the black mills between two hills below me)—
the double-flowering peach, as ancient as the other, and called
"countless-wives, countless-husbands," a colony of red or of white,
producing fruit, and having energy to be lovely, too–an advanced
civilisation—the silver-bell tree and the Judas, thrusting out
                    blossoms
from the blackwood of last year, a pale virginal mist, a disturbing
flame of blood—

          Henry George,
                    I have lain here dreaming,
hearing the whistles and the throbbing of the foundries below me
and as remote as on top of Redondo or the Enchanted Mesa,
in the late April and the early May sun, bathing in it, reading,
talking if I had brought a friend with me, or if the old gardener
chanced my way. There above the stacks and lying on artemisia
50

and on arenaria, I believe I had my first revelation of you.
No doubt
there had been events paving the way; but you are, and always
will be for me,
born out of that wealth of botany and landscape. Here is a
difficult thing
to put into words, and I say nothing of much struggling before
and after
and a strange inner dizziness, out of which I kept clutching
for the warm
symbol of us all, the STATE. But I could not have continued
without you.
Fortified privilege all about, breeds too many doubts in the lonely,
and so do plans of reform born of the envious and their responsible;
and I am of the lonely, and hence the joy of that hour I speak of,
remembering,
which flows richly back through me reading you any time, any where.

The STATE has a sacred physical body
and her sacred physical body is the earth
and for all men is the equal right to the use of the earth;
and something more you made clear to me,
harder to phrase, deep as the blood—
a patriotism born of unbroken communion
with the sun, with the planets,
with the dark nights and the stars through the trees
of one's own landscape.

More than anyone you help me to be
both individual and non-individual;
because of you I have grown very quiet in the deeps of my life.
Feeling the pulse in my wrist
I feel underneath that pulse of personal blood
another pulse deeper than I know.

51

TWO MEMORANDA
1914

I. For My New Born Son

The first music your grandfather heard
was the guns of 1860,
and for you, baby, comes over the sea
the assault of Liege..
                "children waking from sleep
wherein they are much more profoundly involved than we.."

And so you have come, dear son,
and you enter a world more beautiful, truly,
than musician or painter has seen it—
despite Chattanooga, or Homestead, or Liege
as well as because of them, more beautiful.
But I wonder whether I can say to you
what my father said to me:
Love breeds love and hate breeds hate—
                say it to you softly, quietly,
                not to tear you over-hastily from sleep:
Can I put everything in its place for *you*,
baby?

II. For My Fellow Stock-Holders

Ashbel Smith wrote Sam Houston in 1843: "I was at the palace
of St Cloud a few days since.. Louis Philippe is a careful ob-
server of events in Texas..as is also Leopold, King of the Bel-
gians.."

53

And Colonel House wrote the President from Berlin in 1915:
"It seems that every German that is being killed or wounded is
being killed or wounded by an American rifle, shell, or bullet.
I never dreamt before of the extraordinary excellence of our
guns and ammunition..the only ones so manufactured that
their results are deadly.. Affectionately yours.."

And the Colonel wrote the President from London the morning
of the Lusitania:"I have never seen Kew Gardens so beautiful.
The blackbirds were singing, and Sir Edward and I talked of
how different they were to those in far away Texas.."

O blackbirds, sing forever in far away Texas,
sing forever in Kew Gardens, and in the Congo—
but you other blackbirds, singing
                  in Essen and Westphalia
                  in Leeds and Birmingham
                  in Pittsburgh and Gary—
blackbirds singing in your heart and mine,
O my fellow-stockholders in the steel and coal companies,
                  the meat and bread companies—
blackbirds whose song is the profits of human agony,
what can we do about you, what can we do about ourselves?

FRANK HOGAN AND FRED DEMMLER
1918

Doctors, clerks, statisticians: naked men and boys being weighed and measured, having their chests thumped, their hearts listened to: a glance at the eyelids peeled back, a glance at the arches.

Only the best go to the cannons.

The Red Cross is shipping doctors, nurses, internes: shipping surgical instruments, iodine, wooden legs.

Anno Domini 1918 we transport a shell two thousand miles, shoot it a thousand yards into a trench, shoot a human being with it.

If we don't kill the soldier outright, just destroy his leg, or his arm, or his balls, or his eyes, then the surgeons and the knives are at hand to save what is left of him.

* * *

And so the Pittsburgh fellows began to go.

Frank Hogan was in college studying to be a writer, his imagination mad with the human abundance of the city about him and the five mill valleys. Frank went.

Camp Greene, Charlotte, N. C. Nov. 21, 1917—"Of course I said I never would enlist. .and yet the views I expressed I still believe to be correct. I do not believe in the glory of war. I do believe that patriotism is partisanship glorified by nothing. .

55

Heroism is temporary insanity. .cowardice is common sense. . my mind told me that and much more. .and all the time it told me I knew I was going to enlist. .Frank."

Active Service with the A E F, April 29, 1918—"I am now making the grand tour at the expense of the gov't. .my post, I must admit, more insignificant than was fashionable in the days of cultured fraud. The people here are delightful to talk to. .like making a social call at home. .only here one doesn't understand a word of the talk, and at home nobody says anything worth understanding (that is either true or clever, but I hope it isn't true). .I suppose you felt Bob's death as heavily as I did. .we were always together; people used to think of us as brothers. . Frank."

Active Service with the A E F, September 25, 1918—"I was surprised at the way the dead affected me. They lay along the river banks and the woods, one here, three there, in all sorts of odd attitudes. Now and then there would be a dead man by the side of the path on a litter. Some had blood about their nostrils, some had head and shoulders blown away. Yet I had no feeling of horror or even of sympathy. They were not like the dead at home, washed and combed and faultlessly attired in awful dignity amid silks and flowers. The forest was not a death house, but a monstrous wax works; and some of the figures were broken. I remember one man's speaking of the terrible look in the eyes of his friend. It didn't seem that way to me. They were just the blue eyes of a doll that gaze at something a great way off. There was perhaps the suggestion that behind the eyes a soul might still be lurking. But I have always felt that way about the dead. ."

December 30 Captain Bechtold wrote Frank's mother—"Corporal Hogan was advancing in the Argonne Forest on Oct. 6th with his company and was under shell fire and machine gun fire. A machine gun bullet hit him and he died a few minutes later. A brave and true soldier who has given his all to his country.."

The next spring Lieutenant Moore wrote Roland Wilson from Andernach, Germany—"He was buried close to where he fell, a spot slightly south of the town of Clunel.. With greatest uniformity the men of his company characterised him as a first-grade American..game to the core.."

Au revoir, Frank. A Pittsburgh boy with your work ahead,
caught in a nightmare of strands stronger than steel
woven of our human nature through the generations,
a web dooming anyone past hope: you went to your death
in the good cheer of the spirit. As your letters show,
these letters, few, and perfect, "holding the scorn of death
like a flower at the lips"—the scorn of all humbug
and the falseness in the world, and with a little smile,
as though you had knowledge of matters beyond our reach
touching the sacrifice of life and of death,
and the long ages that have been given to sacrifice
in racial, in personal experience, that war may stop—
as though you took no bitter view, but understood
what game of chess life plays against the Shadow,
had calculated the chances of life's winning
in the aeons ahead, and had faith, and were content.
Plastic in the hands of destiny, yielding
the non-individual in you to the non-individual in life
to do with as it pleased, *you* stayed aloof, and smiled.

The soul, supreme:
true, the need of the disappearance of the individual
has come upon us, but never of the individual soul:

gathering a few of your letters here
like a writing of apricot blossoms against a sky
over which a black storm came, fatally,
I salute you.

* * *

Fred Demmler went.

Fred was a painter. He had gone to art school in Boston, and had come home and hired a studio in a building in the thick of Wood Street. He painted portraits of a good many of us there.

The June before the war, his father sent him abroad for further study. His grandfather before coming to America had hoped to be a painter, and now he could be one in his grandson. Which of us can be all he wishes to be in one life time? Fred was to meet Henry James and John Sargent in London, study in Munich, see the galleries of the world. And he was fitted to absorb and value human perspectives and excellences, and then come back to his own life in his own town.

The Archduke was assassinated.

Fred lingered abroad as long as he could. He was in Downing Street the night the cabinet sat waiting for Germany's reply:

"It gave one an odd feeling to realise that behind the drawn shades sat men who were settling the question of life and of death for hundreds of thousands.. The crowd cheered, I did not."

He fell in love with a painting: "In the first room was a portrait of an old woman, painted in his last period. Time after time I went there intending to see the rest of the gallery. Sometimes I even tried a room or two. What was the use? It seemed to me as if the whole history of the human race were concentrated in that old woman's face.."

He had read "The Kingdom of God is Within You," and had understood it, had known why Tolstoy was right that violence is no way to settle a quarrel.

He didn't know what to do about conscription.

"If there were no one but myself to consider.. But the suffering you would have no hesitation in imposing upon yourself you hesitate to impose on those dearer than yourself.."

"The military experts have found a nice polite term for men killed or too badly maimed to fight any more—*wastage*."

"This frantic enthusiasm for democracy..on the part of a people who have spent their whole lives combating it."

He left Pittsburgh for three days in the country. Three days with his ghost, along the banks of the Ohio, or rowing the swift yellow Kanawah.

Then he registered for the draft.

He was soon in France. "I wish you could drop in on me and talk through one of these fine moonlit nights of things and ideas and ideals (aside from military) occupying the thoughts and hopes of men.."

He wrote to one of his friends—"Keep up your good work.. your results are much needed." He wrote to another—"Continue your work..other victories are transient. The faith you have in me (which I prize so desperately) I have in you, no matter where each of us may be headed. We will live the best we can—that, through our friendship, is all we ask of each other."

The sergeant Fred bunked with told Oscar Demmler, later: "He had no buddy, he was everybody's friend."

One of his comrades said, "The transport *Caserta* brought us over—dirty hulk, food rotten, trip rough..Fred the only one that never missed a meal. He never kicked—when we complained about anything he said it would be better later."

Some human beings are not afraid that things can overpower them.

He read the Beatitudes often, and some of the battalion grew fond of them, too. He wondered why ministers didn't preach on the Beatitudes more.

Captain Siddall wrote Alan Bright—"On October 31 our company started over the top at Olsene, Belgium, at 5 a.m. Fred was leading his gun team and had progressed about 150 yards east of the railroad when struck with a piece of H E shell. He was severely wounded in the left side and evacuated to the field hospital.."

General Orders No 86, 37th Division, December 1918: "The Division Commander records his appreciation of the meritorious services of —
   Sergeant Fred A. Demmler (died of wounds)..

* * *

Seventeen years have gone by.
Seventeen years is a long time, to a man alive:
what has happened to you, old crony?
60

I grow more of a crab, no doubt,
though not in my heart. The world is worse since the war:
hate and fear where one expects them least.
                    Not that it matters,
looked at in cycles; the drunken man zigzags homeward, of course.
Fred, what has happened to you?
                    Do you know what God knows, now?
And is the truth different from what the living can catch a glimpse
                    of—
that one must do one's best by the outward world, as neighbor
                    and   citizen;
but that the shortcomings of the real, in which all glides to
                    disorder,
are best healed, considered in ages, by the man who holds
to his own heart and dream: his own heart and dream really being,
from any angle, the reason why the real remains imperfect,
never more significant than a child's book of sketches, random,
a mere hint of what might be in our world..
                    To do one's best
as neighbor and citizen, along with earning the needs
of one's family, meaning to nourish *any* outward manifestation
of the pure and all-healing inward..
                    Is there a way you could tell me,
or is this what you are telling me?

DUSE DIES IN PITTSBURGH

After the world war there was another steel strike, larger than Homestead, and again the strikers lost. And there were strikes over the country like lightning round the entire horizon; and the President tried to find out why, and his committee made a report to him.

It seemed to many Americans that all the problems the committee reported to the President were capable of solution.

At least, if we could learn to go outside ourselves to befriend the leper and then go inside ourselves to befriend the leper, the leper being the same leper.

And the Secretary of Labor came to Pittsburgh and said, "Every man is entitled to the full social value of what his labor produces, of course; but before you put your fine-spun theory into practical operation it would be necessary to devise a method of computation.. The only method we have devised is the method we are using, competition.."

And Bishop Lawrence said to the Diocese of Massachusetts, "The Church has not the spirit of Christ if it does not touch these problems.."

And before he died Franklin K. Lane wrote to a friend, "I deal all day with hard questions of economics, so that I am nothing of a preacher; but I know there will never come anything like peace or serenity by a mere distribution of wealth, although that distribution is necessary and must come.."

And Lenin died.

And thirteen days later Woodrow Wilson died.

And many people grieved, because Lenin and Wilson, each
in his way, had been working at new methods of compu-
tation.

But what grieved me more,
because it implied a still different system of computation
(true, the need of the disappearance of the individual
has come upon us—but never of the individual soul),
was that Duse came to Pittsburgh and died there.

The divine Duse. An old woman then,
but still the most shining woman in the world.

They kept her alive with oxygen in other cities
so she might die in Pittsburgh. Death
had something in mind; brought her the long leagues from Italy
so she might die in my city.
She wouldn't stop in Indianapolis;
said she had heard that "Spittsburgh" was a nice city,
insisted on going through to Spittsburgh,
died there, crying for the boat to take her home.

Duse who, in the agony of the war,
said she would never again play any parts
but those of mothers.
                    The mothers, only the mothers.

It was then she became the divine Duse.

She had acted the passions. She knew how they can destroy the soul of a person and the soul of a world, and she saw that the nations of the earth had reached their black hour.

It was then she became the divine Duse, rose before the nations and showed them the only way out of blackness: became the mothers, left passion behind and lived only for what cherishes.

In the centre of the stage of the world, closing the ring of her thought and feeling, she held aloft the beauty of human life as in a golden cup, and not a drop of it could leak away—

abandoned passion and went forward into what cherishes—

became the grail—

shone forth like a mysterious aureole over the swamps of my city, the swamps of my world, for a moment.

* * *

"I am nothing of a preacher, but I know there will never come anything like peace or serenity by a mere distribution of wealth.."

And the mistake of us who are ardent, is not to see that a system is worth only what the individuals in it are worth, and individuals who have not left passion behind and gone forward into what cherishes, are not worth as much now as they may be later.

May it grow, this nation of ours, this Tree of our life,
        out of our own entrails—
away from envy of the better man,
away from dreams of class, of personal power,
of personal revenge.

To give, to give all, to give all voluntarily:
may it grow from a faith in the usefulness of sacrifice,
in a heaven-born love of one's fellows
and one's native landscape.

"BLOOM FOREVER, O REPUBLIC"
1925

After the steel companies beat the unions at Homestead the officers of the company became the leaders of the workers, having done away with any other leaders.

Once Lincoln Steffens went to see Judge Gary and asked him if that was not the truth, and the President of the steel corporation said he could see "there was something in it."

Steffens wanted to know what Judge Gary as their leader had done for the steel workers. The Judge said the corporation had begun to make them stockholders and had done a good deal of welfare work.

Steffens was not impressed by these methods of "re-peopleising" the country's industries.

From coast to coast, corporations had been selling stock to their employees as well as to their consumers, and a good many other Americans were not impressed. In 1925 the Academy of Political Science had a meeting in New York to find out whether this kind of ownership could prevent the country from continuing to divide into two unfriendly and arrogant camps. Proceedings, March 9, 1925:

Vice President Arthur Williams of the New York Edison Co. said that in 1922 Consolidated Gas had 12,173 stockholders, but in 1925 more than 60,000; and employees to the number of 11,345 and consumers to the number of 25,844 owned the preferred stock.

Vice-President Albert Harris of the New York Central said: "The past winter we undertook to sell New York Central employees New York Central stock. . and 41,500 employees wanted 97,000 shares."

Vice-President Devereux of Bell Telephone Securities said: "At present over 62,500 of our employees are stockholders of record, and 65,700 are purchasing through payroll deductions, and 329,733 Americans own an average of 26 shares apiece."

Herbert C. Pell of the New York Democratic State Committee said that words of such kind to uphold the existing as against the system that preceded it, "sounded very much like the glittering bauble socialists offer us in exchange for our liberty"; that you could not imagine a steel stockholder thrilling with joy at the spectacle of a Chinese carpenter with an American hammer, the way you could Mr Eastman hearing that an Eskimo "had recorded his fiance's charms with a kodak"; that "the new ownership didn't give a damn about anything but profits, and it was no longer shameful for business leaders to race down to Washington screaming for subsidies, which are the whiskey of commerce"; and that "Dr Jekyll found it easier and easier to become Hyde till he had to become Hyde forever."

And Eustace Seligmann of Sullivan and Cromwell said: "Under present business ethics directors frequently profit personally by information which they obtain in their capacity as directors"; and he inquired how you could oust wicked directors when they charge to the company the expense of fighting *you*, and you yourself have to pay for the ways and means of fighting *them*.

Director George H. Soule, Jr., of the Labor Bureau was reminded of neurasthenic people who try to avoid dealing with reality by a substitute that means nothing. "If you want to give your workmen more interest in your establishment, the easy and logical way to do it is to recognise and deal with the organisations they have formed for that purpose."

President Pierrepont B. Noyes of Oneida said that under the present system almost all our surplus billions go to the capitalist class, and labor's share is pitiful; and those in leadership and power "ought to cultivate the ability of putting themselves in the place of the great majority and recognise their need *not* of a certain wage, or a club house, or a playground. ."

Herbert Hoover, Secretary of Commerce, told the conference over the radio:". .for twenty years the national ratio of owned homes has fallen. ."

Henry L. Stimson, Secretary of War, said that the relations between capital and labor, and producer and consumer, were only a modified war; and the Belly and the Members, for all practical purposes, remained a fable still.

Donald R. Richberg, special counsel for the City of Chicago in Public Utility Litigation, said that "the consumer-producer was a myth, and nobody could ride two horses going in opposite directions, and any circus performer could tell you that"; and said also, that "to persuade your customer to buy your stock was as clever and neat an accomplishment as to persuade a marathon runner to carry along refreshments for his competitor." What the new popular ownership came down to was merely "an improvement in the mechanism of minority control," since you could now control a business with a fourth or a fifth of the voting stock.

Proceedings, March 9, 1925. And at the banquet in the evening ex-Justice William L. Ransom quoted what Dean Harlan F.

Stone had said at Cooper Union in 1915: "There is no such thing as rights of property as distinguished from rights of men."

* * *

Whether or no the new popular ownership amounted to much so far as labor was concerned, by this year there was hardly any unionism left in the Pittsburgh district (except for coal and construction), nor in American industry as a whole, for that matter.

It was still the age of Homestead.

A Pittsburgh banker named A. W. Mellon was Secretary of the Treasury. His chief idea was to cut rates of taxation so as to stimulate more productive industries.

Labor (the railway man's weekly) said there were enough productive industries but the masses lacked the purchasing power to keep them busy; and what we needed was more, not less, of redistribution of the national income.

Certain economists said it was an obvious truth. They warned the country it would be wiser to pay off the war debt than to increase expansion in productive industry and unproductive speculation. They said the boiler was on the point of bursting as it was.

The Literary Digest took a popular vote on the Mellon plan, and South Dakota was the only state to reject it. All the others agreed to cut the inheritance tax and the surtaxes, and repeal the capital stock tax and the gift tax. Pennsylvania, New York, and New England endorsed the Mellon plan 80 to 90 percent.

So that the Mellon plan, which was the Pittsburgh plan, the Big Business plan, the Masters' plan in any age or place, was also at that moment the national plan.

70

The Democratic-Progressive coalition fought the Secretary of the Treasury but could not fight the whole country.

It was a moment of terror.

It was like the Black Death in Europe in the XIVth century. We did not die, but something in us was dying. We were forgetting our fellow man.

As a nation we were veering away from constructive change.

We were not listening to the ideals and the religion which inclined us to sympathy with the struggle of the underprivileged.

Great causes were as unheeded as the legend of the Grail.

* * *

There were other "town-meetings" this anxious year. A journal of political economy held a symposium:
Professor Watkins: "On the high tide of prosperity we have all been swept out to sea..adrift without chart, compass, or sextant.. Whither are we going? The only answer from the captains of Big Business is: 'Going on!' Is that enough?"
Mr Filene: "Mass production cannot live under the control of the short-sighted type of business man, but will, by enlightened selfishness, pay high wages and sell for as low as possible, in order to make the greatest possible profits.."
Mr Cravath: "Big Business is a real menace. Yes. But what are you going to do about it? The remedy does not lie in legislation or in the courts or in any attempt of government to force men to act against their wills. In the face of any such attempt the forces of life will be found stronger than the forces of law."

* * *

Three years later R. B. Mellon, former chairman of Pittsburgh Coal, was interrogated by the Senate committee on Interstate Commerce:

Mr Eaton: You have read all about these social conditions among these employees and the terrible destitution, have you not?

Mr Mellon: Yes.

Mr Eaton: It has been spread broadcast in the public press.

Mr Mellon: Yes.

Mr Eaton: What have you ever done to alleviate these conditions?

Mr Mellon: O there are a number of charities and schemes of different kinds. They have been taken care of. I think they have been well taken care of all during the winter.

Senator Wheeler: You think these striking miners and their families have been well taken care of?

Mr Mellon: I think so, from what they tell me.

Senator Wheeler: You have not seen any of them, have you?

Mr Mellon: No; I did not go out to see them. I would not be out there, way out in the mines.

Senator Wheeler: Well, if you think they are being well taken care of, Mr Mellon, it would do you good to go out there and see them for yourself.

"I would not be out there, way out in the mines." The average stockholder in a company naturally has to take much for granted.

"Big Business is a real menace."

Even a store at a country cross-roads is a real menace, when it is inhuman.

72

The governor of Pennsylvania, Gifford Pinchot, said in his Farewell address in 1927: "Politics in this state has been run as a part of the business of certain moneyed interests. These interests invest in politics as they do in mills or mines or banks, and for the same purpose—to make money... What these interests buy is non-interference, tax exemption, extortionate rates allowed public utilities and other special privileges for themselves at the expense of the people."

At the expense of the people—

because we the people do nothing about it—

forget that the country is ours, and there is no such thing as the rights of property as distinguished from *our* rights.

* * *

And yet, the State is the body of which we are the cells,
the State is the armature our private nerves loop back to:
the haunting idea of the State, the bitter need of the State,
it is this that causes the hallucinations and disease
of modern man, causes our soul-sickness and despair
when we go to the polls and vote, even when the election
is fraudulent, and the candidates vile.

Louis XIV said *I am the State*, and Jay Gould said *The public be damned*, and H. C. Frick said *We propose to manage our own business as we think proper and right.*

And once Verestschagin the painter visited Scarsdale and said to Kate, then very much the young lady as she told me: "And do you like Twilight Park?" (that being an amusement place), and she said, "Yes, I love it; but I loathe the people there."

73

And he stood enormously over her, beetling his brows: "Be sure, my dear, that they reciprocate."

What causes our hallucinations and disease is the belief that we can get to work on the State without getting to work on ourselves.

> "Man is the wildfire out of the planet"—
> man is one kind of wildfire, anyway:
> and have you seen what plays about the silver and
>   platinum helmets
> of Rainier and Shasta, in the moonlight?
> It is a different fire: but Lincoln and Whitman
> are as unearthly, are as luminous—
> *With charity towards all, with malice towards none..*
> *When I give, I give myself..*
>   are as unearthly:
> and so is anybody yielding his life for another,
> or to gain more life for us all.

When we received the death-lists from the Argonne, Mrs Hogan (Frank's mother) called me to her house and gave me the books Frank liked and read most, among them Whitman's Prose, conned and re-conned; and I paid attention to the passages Frank had marked, among others this one:

"Beyond the independence of a little sum laid aside for burial money and of a few clapboards around and shingles overhead on a lot of American soil own'd.., the melancholy prudence of the abandonment of such a great being as man is, to the toss and pallor of years of money-making..stifling deceits and underhand dodgings..shameless stuffing while others starve.. ghostly chatter of a death without serenity or majesty..(this) is the great fraud upon modern civilisation and forethought,

74

blotching the surface and system which civilisation undeniably
drafts.."

"Bloom forever, O Republic, from the dust of my bosom."

Yes, from the dust of this bosom,
From the dust of all such bosoms.

* * *

Ly Pittsburgh is the aureole of Duse.

It is the black and red, never-to-be-forgotten sunset of Stephen Foster.

It is an exhibition of heirlooms at Bellefield School. (Children of immigrants brought them. Mary Parker said her grandfather brought the lace mantilla from Spain, and her grandfather's name was Ramon Perce. Marie Jedlicka brought a painted doll made in Bohemia. Giulia di Paolo brought a cut-work cover; she said her mother made it when they lived in Venice.)

It is the workman who said to Carnegie: "It wasn't a question of dollars. The boys would have let *you* kick them, but they wouldn't let that other man stroke their hair."

It is Carnegie sending Frick a message, "I am getting on in years. I'd like to shake hands with you before I die."

It is Frick's reply, "Tell Mr Carnegie that I'll see him in hell."

It is Berkmann saying when they deported him in 1919, nineteen days after Frick's death: "Anyway, Frick left the country before I did."

It is 7689 new pipe organs in the world, 2811 new public libraries. (And if a man sneer at these gifts, what has *he* given back?)

77

It is John Brashear, writing in a letter: "To-morrow evening is Christmas eve and the newsboys celebrate, and are always given sweaters, shoes, caps, and a box of candy. I have been making the speech to them for eighteen years."

It is Charley's boss, telling him one night by the little gate into the Eliza furnaces (I was there and heard him): "You'll find as you grow older money is the thing that talks, that'll buy you a wife, congress, anything.. If you've money, you're right there; if you haven't, you can get out."

It is Herbert Spencer, after Carnegie took him through the mills, "A month in Pittsburgh would justify anyone in committing suicide."

It is Judge Gary endlessly repeating: "As heretofore publicly and repeatedly stated, our corporation and subsidiaries although they do not combat the labor unions as such, decline to discuss business with them.."

It is Frick saying to President Wilson's emissary, with whom also Judge Gary declined to discuss business: "If the President in the honorable conduct of the war has authorised you to ask me as a private citizen to state the cost of ship plates, I can answer his question, and will."

It is Gary at a banquet: "We cannot keep the rates of labor down if competitors are willing to pay higher wages."

It is a Pittsburgh boy writing from camp to a friend who had just been drafted: "There is no formula to follow for the perfect in this new environment, unless it be to enter into the open and generous spirit. Whatever I feel, comes from a sense of responsibility to myself, a faith in myself, above all an abiding hope for better days to come."

78

It is a Pittsburgh girl who said one night when the moon made
a silver web of a young tree outside the window, glistening from
the shower: "There isn't a thing in this damned country you
can be devoted to. Civilisation? only our assembled dumbness."

It is another Pittsburgh girl, and what she said was: "When I
hear some people talk, it seems my early years I was blindfolded
on purpose to feel through my heart and body the things that
do not come with learning."

My Pittsburgh is all these people, and others too;
my Pittsburgh is more than I can ever say—
the people, and the buildings, and the streets
in which I live my life; the loneliness
of heart and body here; the mind's confusion;
the evening pools of light in living rooms;
the conversation, the strange flow of words,
the inward hesitations and delays,
the phantom steel mills floating in these words,
phantom statistics—all reality
become abstract, unless I see revealed
some human destiny in particular,
how such a one is, or is not, defended
against the outward by something in his spirit:
phantoms again, the phantoms of the spirit
against the world's.
                    And so, if someone plays
the violin, or sings a song (of Brahms, say—
Love is Forever, say)
the Pittsburgh vistas change to farther vistas,
the personal conflicts to much mightier conflicts,
and God still lives and therefore we can live,
and can continue, each of us in his way,
the business of self-shaping; can continue

the search for water, which explorers know,
being now ourselves explorers and the world
living within us even more than round us.
Our human speech is merely reticence
and each of us conceals the need of all,
the universal secret,
to feel more clearly our full human stature,
the harmony, the music, we might be.
Water unquiet from the gusts that strike it,
the outward stays disordered from the inward;
this need of ours to grow into our future,
to heal the wound of living and of dying,
how should we fail it, then?

               We shall not fail it:
Can an oak tree be full grown by the seventh day?
The great new sun, the sun of our life together,
is hardly yet at rising; we are men
peering about us in the dark of dawn.

We shall not fail it. We begin to see
new meaning in the pictures of our darkness,
and the half-shadowed figures whom we watch
tell us the truth, and there's no other truth.
Even the mistakes we make in our unfolding
must light the way, and there's no other hope;
there's only lust for self and power besides,
and after that, neurosis, and decay,
and death.

        The great man sees how limbs and leaves
come out of a tree, and he knows.
                   He sees a dancer
braiding one poise with another on the tight-rope,

80

braiding equivalences out of leanings
to left and right, in the great calm of balance,
and he knows.   He gives me his hand and you
his hand, and somewhat his greatness overflows,
steadying us and germinating in us.
His growing warms our growing, and his life
is ours: he crowns us; rather, because of him,
the chrism is on us.   And the future city
lies in the future of its least citizen;
its least citizen is bound by tears and blood
to its greatest citizen, and tears and blood
outlast the firmament. In our confusion
some things are not confused. We only grow
by answering to the eternal and then answering,
with something of the eternal, to ourselves.

* * *

Chrysanthemums blossom, feeling the white frost near them;
but a man need not wait in his stillness to hear death coming
before he take oath that all love is mother-love and a cherishing
or not useable, full of venom. The weeds in us thrive too well;
and till we be made new in love, can we arraign the State
we are the stems and seed of, for the complex ancient nettles
which strangle the future? In this field of smart and sting,
this world of the State we all of us make, only a new spirit
can stop the thieving of sunlight from the defenceless.
How then: what theory of the State can save us,
if we must change the worst in ourselves?

* * *

Stems of a living forest,
Pittsburgh men and women and children,

their roots laced together under the earth,
their branches tied and meshed against the sky—
I have seen those trunks and leaves against the
                    smoking sunsets.

And if you have ever been deep in the plexus of yourself,
you have been deep in the plexus of this forest;
and if thought like a bewildered bird flies down the leafy
                    avenues and finds no way out,
it is too bad for the thought, but it is as well for the heart.

Fear can leap like lightning from stem to stem,
loneliness can tremble in branch after branch,
but so can a hunger for Something Else.

It is too bad for thought, but it is as well for the heart.
The heart that knows the hunger for something Beyond
will know what to do about the fear and loneliness
                    in the fluttering stems and sheaths.

A great wind searches into the wilderness in each of us
                    we call the soul.
There are age-long memories, age-long endurances,
                    in these trees.
The best thing about a forest is the way the Beyond enters it.

* * *

I see the yeast mantle, I hear the yeast murmur
with the violence of the future that agitates it,
with what lies at the root of the future agitating it.

The ferment troubled with untellable germs
murmurs, mantles: the germs of health

fight the germs of disease: in me, in my city
death fights life.

When darkness falls upon democracy
the fault is the majority's. Any way you put it,
a city belongs to the majority.
The way of political action still remains,
the power of a minority to leaven a majority
                                        still remains.

We germs have many lives.
Corpuscles die, corpuscles get better, are reborn,
                                        transformed;
majorities can become minorities.
Blood must course through the whole body,
work and happiness thorugh the whole nation.
                        Science
teaches its lesson with a ruthless quiet,
teaches alike democrat aristocrat socialist fascist,
giving each the choice for the children of life or death.

Does one instruct an embryo in the matter of its growth?

Humility and brotherly love
and a knowledge of corporations
and a knowledge of mass production
and a recollection of the ancient truths
and thoughtful watching of how a good vine bears its grapes—
these are to be among the guides for action.

And our increasing knowledge of what happens
when a man lets himself be mastered by things and events,
when he fails to assert the spirit of his life:
our increasing reverence for the mystery within us—

this, I think, may lead at last to our union
with science and with religion.

* * *

A city finds life when a human being
finds life, when he learns how to walk between
forgetting and remembering the self.

Once I came home to Pittsburgh in September,
came from the west and looked across the river
at the city in the smoke and ninth-month fog.
Tops reached up from the heavy sea of vapor,
the water-towers like minarets, the stacks
with smoke bubbling from them as water bubbles
from upright pipes, and steadily floating south.
Across that unseen river was my city:
bridge-spans, and gaunt black gables, a hill
and on it the campanile of a church:
under the undulations of the vapor
hints of a vast crowding of rigid shapes,
rectangular, implacable, soft only
in the mist which softens all: hints of a vast
ferment of living seed within those shapes.
Despite the horrors of my time, I knew
(and knew it with the greatest joy life gives),
that there were people in that hidden city
seeking the laws of life, mingling their knowledge,
suffering but finding peace in one another,
and learning more and more not to wish power
over anyone but themselves.
                              It was no dream,
those living people, minds and hearts and bodies.

Always the change and interchange of our essence,

the conveyance of our spirit into flesh,
loaded with death if we will, or sweet with life—
in industry and commerce, schools or churches,
at the City Hall, or at home, there is nothing else,
now and forever. And the old-time dreams,
spawn of the shadows of the Napoleon-man,
dissolve before me as sea-mist at sunrise.

We in whose life the seed of seeds is waiting,
what reference have we to created things?
The paths of life are interwoven lives;
we have more reference than we can imagine.
Now we are all explorers, and exploring
for a vision of our life, what is a city?
Pittsburghers, what is Pittsburgh? It is the total
of the relationships of us who live
in Pittsburgh: is nothing else, now and forever.

And it can be reciprocalness in growth.
And it can be accordances of being.
And it can be an unfolding all together.

* * *

NOTES

ACKNOWLEDGMENT: the Stephen Fo&st;er memorandum has appeared in *Scribner's Magazine;* portions of the Henry George and the Epilogue in *The Forum;* Mrs Soffel and Frank Hogan and Fred Demmler in *Space;* and Home&st;ead, Brashear, The Portent, We&st;inghouse, Duse Dies in Pittsburgh, and portions of the Prologue and Epilogue, in *The Survey Graphic.*

AUTHORITIES:

> *The Pittsburgh Survey*
> Berkmann, *Prison Memoirs of an Anarchist*
> Bridge, *The Inside Story of the Steel Trust*
> Carnegie, *Autobiography*
> Carnegie, *The Gospel of Wealth*
> Consensus, *Economic Club of New York, April 1929*
> George, H. Jr., *Life and Letters of Henry George*
> Harvey, *Life and Times of Henry Clay Frick*
> Hay, John, *Journal*
> *The Intimate Papers of Colonel House*
> James, *The Raven: A Biography of Sam Houston*
> *The Letters of Franklin K. Lane*
> Leupp, *George Westinghouse*
> Mellon, Andrew, *The People's Taxation*
> Milligan, *Stephen C. Foster*
> Muzzey, *History of the United States*
> Nevin, *Memoir of Stephen C. Foster*
> O'Connor, *Mellon's Millions*
> Price, *Immortal Youth: A Memoir of Fred Demmler*
> *Proceedings of the American Academy of Political Science, XI, 3*
> Scaife, *Life and Letters of John A. Brashear*
> *Social Progress, A Handbook of the Liberal Movement*
> Steffens, *Autobiography*
> Thayer, *Life of John Hay*
> Winkler, *Incredible Carnegie*

The account of Mrs Soffel comes from newspapers of the time. Copies of Frank Hogan's letters and those of his officers came to me from Rowland Wilson, and the third letter appears in The Soldier's Progress, an anthology of the war letters of Carnegie Tech men. Mo&st; of the quotations from Demmler's letters come from the Memoir by Lucien Price. The letters of his officers and the comments of his fellow soldiers came to me from Oscar Demmler.

ABOUT THE AUTHOR

Born the son of missionary parents in Rangoon, Burma, Haniel Long (1888–1956) moved to Pittsburgh when he was three. One of his first memories was of the Homestead strike, when his father removed the pews from his church so that it could accommodate the homeless. Long was ten when his family left Pittsburgh, but he lived in the city intermittently for about twenty years, and in the 1920s he taught English at the Carnegie Institute of Technology (now Carnegie Mellon University).

In 1929 he moved to Santa Fe, where he became the guiding force of a writers' colony that included Oliver La Farge, Paul Horgan, and Frieda Lawrence. They formed the imprint of Writers' Editions and defined themselves as "a cooperative group of writers living in the Southwest, who believe that regional publication will foster the growth of American literature."

Haniel Long published many other books, including *Poems* (1920), *Notes for a New Mythology* (1926), *Atlantides* (1933), *Interlinear to Cabeza De Vaca* (1936), *Walt Whitman and the Springs of Courage* (1938), *Malinche* (1939), *The Grist Mill* (1945), and *Spring Returns* (posthumously, 1958). His work also appeared in such magazines as *Fantasy, Commonweal, Scribner's* and *The New Republic.*

Pittsburgh Memoranda was first published in 1935 in a limited edition of 1000 copies signed by the author. The book was composed, printed, and bound by The Rydal Press, Santa Fe, for Writers' Editions. The present edition is an exact facsimile of the first, except for changes to the title page and copyright page, the omission of the limited edition notice, and the addition of this information about the author.